the past is a jean jacket

the past is a jean jacket

Cloud Delfina Cardona

HUB CITY PRESS
SPARTANBURG, SC

Book design: Kate McMullen
Cover images via
Cloud Delfina Cardona
Unsplash
Texture Fabrik
Author Photo: Andres Cardona

Executive Director, Publisher: Meg Reid
Managing Editor: Kate McMullen
Marketing Assistant: Julie Jarema
Editor: Katherine Webb-Hehn
Poetry Series Editor: Jae Nichelle
Editor-at-large: Ashley M. Jones

Type: Baskerville 10/13.5
Display: Clash Display

Library of Congress Cataloging-in-Publication Data

Names: Cardona, Cloud Delfina, 1994- author
Title: The past is a jean jacket / Cloud Delfina Cardona.
Other titles: Past is a jean jacket (Compilation)
Description: Spartanburg, SC : Hub City Press, 2025.
Series: Hub City Press BIPOC Poetry Series
Identifiers: LCCN 2025018924 (print)
LCCN 2025018925 (ebook)
ISBN 9798885740593 (paperback)
ISBN 9798885740630 (epub)
Subjects: LCGFT: Poetry
Classification: LCC PS3603.A73537 P37 2025 (print)
LCC PS3603.A73537 (ebook)
DDC 811/.6—dc23/eng/20250418
LC record available at https://lccn.loc.gov/2025018924
LC ebook record available at https://lccn.loc.gov/2025018925

Epigraph from *Amapolasong* by Jacinto Jesús Cardona.
Used by permission of Plancha Press.

HUB CITY PRESS
153 N Spring Street
Spartanburg, SC 29306
1.864.577.9349

could i be the bookish bato?

—Jacinto Jesús Cardona

table of contents

1 the past is a jean jacket
3 self portrait as an Anna Karina GIF at 17
5 i feel like an Antonioni Movie
7 underneath Catholic all girls' high school in San Antonio, Texas
9 sleepover-shape
11 filth-shaped
12 what i know
14 when i hear "I am my ancestors' wildest dream"
16 eternal life
17 tía-shaped
20 i am always busy wanting other lives
22 indie sleeze hauntology
23 Self Portrait as a Lana del Rey "Born to Die" Music Video GIF at 18
24 ghosting my past selves
25 sometimes it strikes me and my body is on fire
26 ours poetica (or i love triggering myself)
27 Gender Shape
28 gender-shape #2
30 self portrait as my memory of nana's backyard
32 sky
34 Having a Lone Star with You
35 constellation-shape
36 witness

37 gender-shape #3
38 reflecting on a butch's tattoo in the chinese takeout line
40 summer on w. summit
41 unbury the light
43 september 2021
44 black stones
45 La Lechuza at Woodlawn Lake Park
47 january 2018
48 central texas seance
51 friend-shape
52 i've been meaning to
53 flower talk
54 picking up margarita mix on new year's eve
56 like a hot tortilla on the comal, my brain bloats with longing
58 love poem
59 apology to my past selves

61 Notes
62 Acknowledgements

the past is a jean jacket

do you ever forget
who you are
until someone else says your name?

sometimes
i'm so lonely
i practice
small talk
in my car
sometimes i talk to myself
all serious
updating me
about my latest tragedy

most times
it makes me laugh
i can be so dramatic

my bad habit is
looking through
photos
i make visits
to all my past selves

my oversized jean jacket
and velvet ballet flats
pins that announce
my coolness
trying to be
whatever it was
i thought
the room wanted me to be

at night i close my eyes
and walk into rooms
i find myself at the pool table
losing horribly to You

You are singing a James Brown song
on the touchtunes jukebox
The song i picked
is twenty minutes out
it plays long after i leave

i don't notice that i left
i spend the night looking for myself
in the backseat
in the street
in the backyard
of our friend's house
i am nowhere to be found.

self portrait as an Anna Karina GIF at 17

"The more one talks, the less the words mean"
—Vivre Sa Vie

i want a black bob & French fluency
like Anna Karina

i want to look melancholy
in a seductive type of way

instead I have Bright Eyes lyrics
tangled in my hair

& dried blood
around my cuticles

i spend my weekends lassoing
glossy pictures of Audrey Tatou & Thom Yorke

whiteness scotch taped to blue walls
i want to believe my face will change

a friend cuts my bangs
& it does nothing

my round face mocks me my brain
is steeped in Belle & Sebastian

my wanting for black & white bike
rides & cigarettes is never-ending

i avoid eye contact with myself but spend
time in the mirror of *Ghost World*

why does my sadness feel
so ordinary

when i get home from school
i suck up time, wake from naps

to the sound of oven exhaust
arroz con pollo

i sit with my family
in silence

i feel like an Antonioni Movie

i run like the curly haired children do.
my body adorned in white linen,

hair pulled back into a ponytail with wispy bangs
concealing my dark eyebrows.

i press my torso up against the open window pane
and cradle my face with my hand while the camera

cuts to a man on a bike that i'm in love with.
he wears faded white shirts and black shoes.

he brakes outside my apartment. i say his name
and it's as smooth as wedding cake.

we agree to meet in alleyways at night,
cobblestones baptized with leftover rain.

it would sort of be like my first kiss.
we were fourteen and made out in the dark

walkway of the Quarry movie theater.
i stayed up late, wondering:

how does anything ever get done
when kissing exists?

when he broke up with me two weeks later, i cried
my pointy eyeliner off in a pile of dirty laundry.

i threw away stories i wrote about our wedding,
how we would tell our children we were both named after

Italian movie stars, how i would show our kids *Cinema*
Paradiso like my father did that one afternoon.

he turned up the volume to hear the Ennio Morricone score
over the air conditioner's whir while

i watched the montage of black-and-white kisses.
my small heart, like an earthquake in a jar,

learned that movies could love me back.

underneath Catholic all girls' high school in San Antonio, Texas

after francine j. harris

10,000 multi-colored maxi pad wrappers

5,000 shiny lavender plastic tampon applicators

crumpled up copies of the order of the mass

balled up Taco Cabana aluminum foil

Spanish tests with low grades from the Tejanas

French tests with high grades from the fresas

shamrock-shaped paper cutouts
with the names of ivy leagues

broken plaid headbands
too many hair ties to count

oil blotting sheets for greasy girls

mismatched knee high socks

hair straighteners forgotten after graduation

notes from girls who want to know
what it is like to be with another girl

notes about making plans to meet up
behind the science building

notes from girls who weren't sure if friendship
was supposed to be full of longing

the sort of love that is buried in dirt,
silent and unknown as a jewel

sleepover-shape

we sit in dewy grass
while night bruises blue

"Linger" by The Cranberries
echoes from her iPod Touch

each cell flipped over like
pancakes my grandfather made

by the Gulf of Mexico
back before we were ideas

in our parents' minds
we lie in her backyard trampoline

while other girls talk of God
Radiohead's guitars from "High and Dry"

speak to us like tarot cards
Seven of Cups Reversed

her hands brush the pleats
of my blue dress and i can't stop

feeling like i wish i was born
with different sins in November

in another blue dress
The Virgin Suicides

soundtracks our first kiss
her purple walls and skylight

baptizes us indigo
time turns into dust

on the car ride home
with my mother's silence

i feel the ghost
of her mouth on mine

i want to feel
anything else

yesterday's desire drips
out of my pores

while the afternoon's hours
wash my room with gray light

until everything is shadow on the
television Jean Seberg says

I'm shutting my eyes tight
so everything goes

black. But I can't do it.
It's never entirely black.

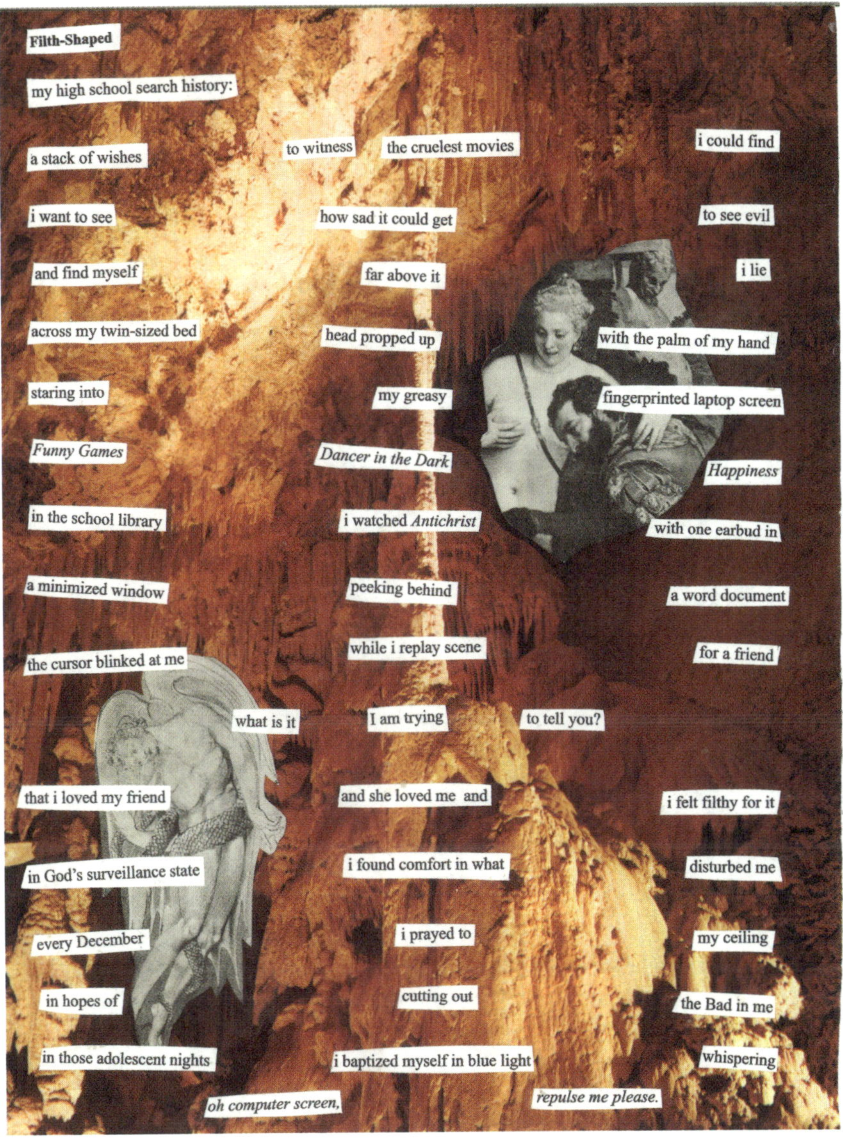
Filth-Shaped
my high school search history:
a stack of wishes to witness the cruelest movies i could find
i want to see how sad it could get to see evil
and find myself far above it i lie
across my twin-sized bed head propped up with the palm of my hand
staring into my greasy fingerprinted laptop screen
Funny Games *Dancer in the Dark* *Happiness*
in the school library i watched *Antichrist* with one earbud in
a minimized window peeking behind a word document
the cursor blinked at me while i replay scene for a friend
what is it I am trying to tell you?
that i loved my friend and she loved me and i felt filthy for it
in God's surveillance state i found comfort in what disturbed me
every December i prayed to my ceiling
in hopes of cutting out the Bad in me
in those adolescent nights i baptized myself in blue light whispering
oh computer screen, *repulse me please.*

what i know

all i know about tío Raul and bisabuela Jesusita
is from the warped mirrors of loved ones.

sometimes i wish i could rip the veil
between this world and the next

i want to ask my tío about the time he met ?
and the Mysterians. i want to look at my bisabuela

while she tells me about her childhood in Hondo.
i want to know them myself. all I know

is from stray photos tucked away
in my family's dresser. my uncle's blurry

pictures of Cher drag show in the middle
of a Houston mall. Jesusita with her white

curls against the blue couch sprawling
with fields of gray floral print.

i know they would
love me but would they like me?

today, all i know is emails and waiting
while quackgrass sprouts outside

between slabs of southside cement.
all i know is that i miss

everything i don’t know. i take in
the brief silence in my classroom

and wait to hear the unfamiliar
whispers of antepasados—

when i hear "I am my ancestors' wildest dream"

i pray to a closested
lesbian in Northern Mexico

married, with daughters she loved
she felt happiest in the afternoons

with her sisters and comadres
thinking, *couldn't it always be like this?*

i pray to a woman in Piedras Negras,
scrubbing stains while her sister helps out

her friend comes over with her newborn,
they talk about their husbands and drink cafecitos.

long skirts and white blouses.
yes, when i think of my ancestors'

wildest dreams,
i see a crossdressing witch

exiled from her small town.
her walls stained with copal smoke.

why call on ancestors who want
to condemn you if they really knew you?

i want to find the loneliest person
in my lineage and pray to them instead.

i will to erect a statue and leave
them flowers, dress them in a short sleeve

shirt, buttoned all the way to the top.
i will read them *Stone Butch Blues*

and play Fiona Apple songs on my phone.
i will kiss their feet and talk to them

on shadowless days in the fall, i will
keep coming until they answer back.

eternal life

i was taught that it was a gift. a privilege
afforded to the well-behaved. i pictured
day after day in the clouds, running
out of things to do.
how was this supposed to be
a gift? i used to stay up
staring at dusty plastic blinds, spiraling
about living in endless light.
i tried to ignore the sinking
feeling, the unsatisfactory answer
i got from Internet Explorer.
some ideas are too big
for our brains to wrap around.
i kept my fears wrapped
up inside me. i pictured time
slinking off each step into the dark
ahead of me. my adolescent bedtime
ritual meant movie time
in my brain—made up images
of funeral speeches and waxy
bodies of loved ones. i counted all
the ghosts i was bound to meet,
mourning the living while
stray dogs wandered through
the neighborhood. how i envied
their circling of broken sidewalks,
their sleeping on sun-stained grass.
i envied their obscurity
of what i wished
was obscured
in me.

tía-shaped

tía Daniela has a Depeche Mode rose tattooed above her ankle

tía Hortensia moves from pot to pot across her backyard,
begonias, hibiscus, and gardenias anointed with holy hose water

tía Janie tells stories of young white men asking her to
two-step at Cowboys Dance Hall

tía Susan makes the sign of the cross every time
she drives by a Catholic church

tía Cindy says *aver* while she puts on reading glasses to
look at a photo of your novio

tía Rosie watches *Sex in the City* reruns on E! before bed

the tías in tía Maria's family wish she wouldn't stay
with her alcoholic mentiroso husband

tía Lilianna and her "amiga" were the first lesbians you ever saw

tía Rafa drives up from the valley every year for fiesta
she hasn't missed it in sixteen years

tía Andrea isn't really your *tía* tía but she always bought you
what you wanted from Target

tía Blanca washes all of Sunday's dishes while
the Cowboys' commentary rolls on and on and on

tía Adela went back to school despite her Tías giving her shit
about not staying home with her two kids

tía Nayeli is called sensitive because she calls out
homophobic comments from her elder tías

tía Rosie still wears the discontinued powder
she sold in her Avon days

tía Xiomara cuts her friends' hair in her kitchen while
Sábado Gigante fills the silences

tía Dulce sells teas and fajas from the trunk of her toyota camry

tía Antonia gathers her sister's kids to get Dairy Queen
and go honking for the Spurs downtown

tía Carmen ran away from home and her tías say she went on
tour with Mötley Crüe

you love how tía Vicky's peach fuzz halos her face
in the living room's yellow light

tía Denise's San Antonio southside inflection is magic to you,
especially when she starts her sentences with *DUDEEEEE it's*
cause like…

tía Angie lives for the motorcycle breeze that whips
around her on the nighttime highway

tía Sara kicks everyone out of the kitchen while she prepares for
the family's Pay-Per-View backyard pachanga

tía Eva paints portraits of Marilyn Monroe in calavera makeup
with a banner that reads, *Smile Now, Cry Later*

every señora who calls you *mija* is your tía

every woman who has ever offered you a tampon is your tía

every west side butch4butch couple you see in public are your tías

when someone splinters your blood, a million tías spill out

when the gods tire of their stars, they will create a new galaxy of
tía-shaped constellations

when i am dust-shaped, let me be remembered like
a niece's favorite tía

when i am dust-shaped, let me be remembered like
a black sheep tía

when i am dust-shaped, let me be remembered like a tía
in a foldable chair by the Gulf of Mexico, squeezing a lime
into her beer while the sun kisses her Deftones tattoo

i am always busy wanting other lives

at sixteen, i aspired to be
a Mexican-American Margot Tenenbaum

reading J.D. Salinger in the bathtub.
i took so many photos of myself

in the hope of finding someone else.
i stare at the shape of my mouth

and find my father.
i stare at my silhouette and find

a matriarchal lineage of longing.
i feed pennies to the cosmic

wishing well every night,
and ask for a sliver of what it is

like to embody want.
i wish i was the type

of person who says, *i don't care*
what other people think,

and actually means it.
i don't like admitting

that white propaganda
had caked itself onto my teenage brain.

like a life-long sunburn,
i am peeling a little more every day.

once i swang at the Barbie-shaped
piñata while my tío tugged at the rope.

her yellow, tissue-paper hair rustled in the hot
March air while the next kid cracked

her rib cage open. my brown friends
and cousins watched her hemorrhage

with strawberry candy
we ate all week long—

indie sleeze hauntology

i used my tv like a crystal ball watching *Submarine.*

i wanted to summon a soundtracked life and long bangs.

alone in my bedroom, i looked at Flickr accounts

crowded with pale teenagers in forests, at beaches,

at parties holding PBR cans, mourning a future that

would be over before i could be one of them. i went to

Ross and Marshall's with my mom in search of the

perfect powder blue Zooey Deschanel dress. i listened to

britpop, watched *Skins* and read *Go Ask Alice*, borrowed

from my best friend. we bonded over glamorizing

addiction, thinking we weren't really living

our lives yet. we were hothouse flowers but still fantasized

about our lives post college, listening to Animal Collective looking

at our Tumblr archive full of volkswagen vans and galaxy prints.

what i want to ask is how do you grieve an impossible life?

Self Portrait as a Lana del Rey "Born to Die" Music Video GIF at 18

i watch this video on my baby blue sheets
after walking home from the dentist.
i brand myself as a teenage intellectual,
but really i am just depressed.
i watch Lana Del Rey's
live performances and laugh
while i was really
Lana Del Rey-ing my way through high school—
listening to Leonard Cohen
before creative writing
longing for an older man's attention, romanticizing
mental illness on my Tumblr. maybe my repulsion
was just projection—this was all before i had language i needed,
before i knew beneath the disgust
is really just desire—
i feel so alone on a Friday night
pretending to be someone i'm not
feeling dramatic at sunset.
we aren't so unalike
we love to live in the wound,
circling sentences
in Sylvia Plath's journal like:

My consuming interest in men and their lives
is often misconstrued as a desire to seduce them
or an invitation to intimacy.

our sadness feels the same, but do the raw edges
of your fingers catch on the satin sheets?

ghosting my past selves

my friend and i talk about the past,
asking each other *do you ever feel*
like you don't know who you are?
yes oh my god yes
how do you resolve the person you were
into the person you are? the complete disconnect—
i don't know how to forget who i was,
haunted by the self in a thrifted black velvet
blacking out on a 4loko, listening to
teen suicide and getting over
months of head lice.
all the selves i've shoved
to the bottom of a well,
leaning over the table
waiting for a kiss
never to come.

sometimes it strikes me and my body is on fire

the way i spend my days
is the way i spend my life

sometimes i can't get over it

my life has been going on
this whole time

not everything is the jukebox
on South LBJ Drive

not everything is the small patio
at the one bedroom apartment,

not everything is the night
with all your friends at the rooftop bar,

chain smoking until you're somehow back
at your old apartment again

watching your friend roll cigarettes
listening to "Zurich is Stained" by Pavement

to be honest, i wasn't even my happiest in
these times. why am i nostalgic for

the shitty times in my life? nostalgic for
addiction? addicted to nostalgia?

i hate using these vague words like addiction
and nostalgia. i've been taught to show, not tell.

but i need to ask you this: how do you accept
that your life is your life?

ours poetica (or i love triggering myself)

for my girls and gays

like a never-ending cake we layer our memories
on top of each other—diner coffee and February hours
at the public library—afternoons where we got stuck
in emo chords—Sunday morning rituals of hangover breakfast
specials at Hermano's—shedding last night's details from our shoulders—
trying our best to punish ourselves for no reason at all

today, grease stains blossom in the chip basket
we flip through yellow menus with cropped pixelated
pictures of Jarrito flavors y lunch specials
we sip from big red plastic cups—we talk about our
boredom of POC narratives that center whiteness
top 40 reggaeton fills in the gaps between our sentences

we sit in the car for over an hour in the parking lot
alternating between laughing and crying
Yo La Tengo on low volume—the sky turns cornflower
and that's when we know it's time to go but first
we step out to pull cards by the river where it's almost too dark to see

we make fun of ourselves and our mental illnesses after
watching Sasha Colby whip her hair to Paramore—we joke
about wanting to die—we document our depressive episodes in
our poems and songs like telephone wire against gray sky—you
send me a message that says *i love*
triggering myself i say *that's a poem title bro*

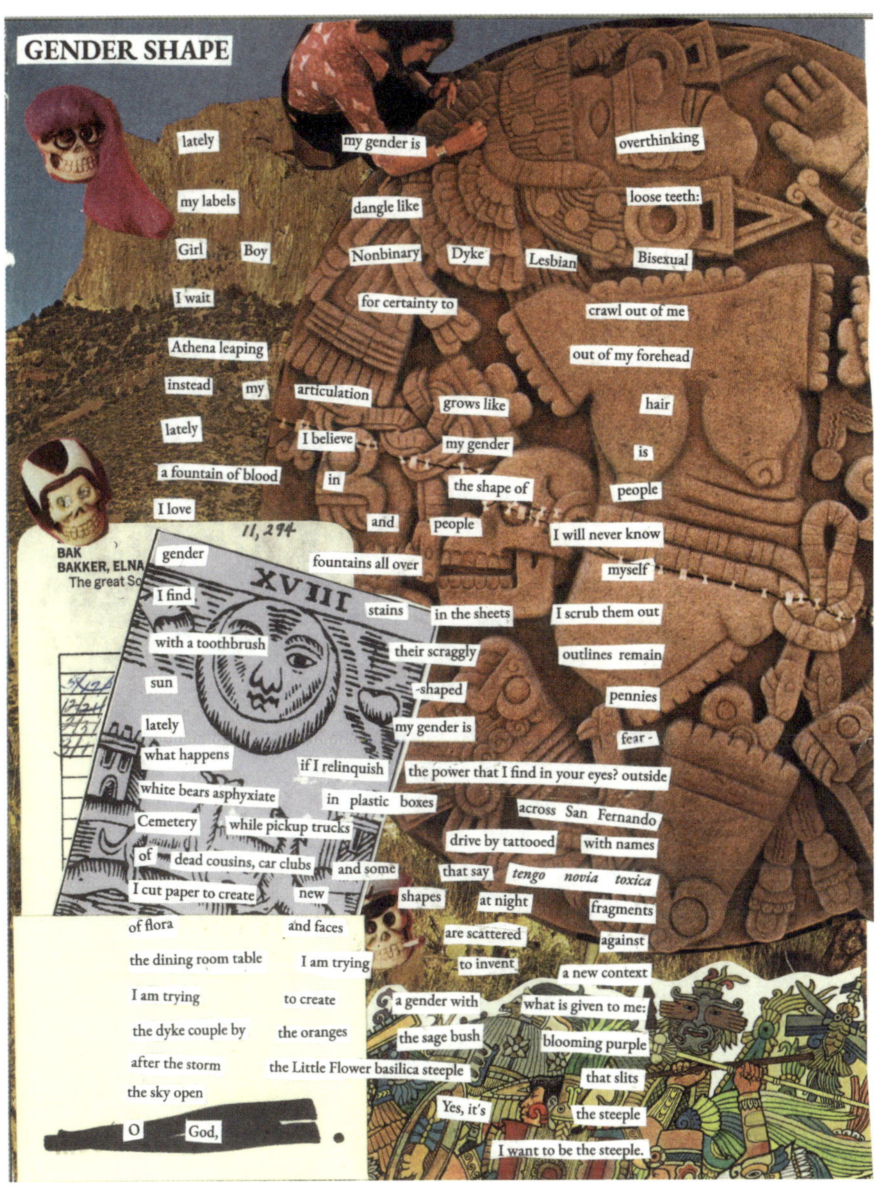
GENDER SHAPE
lately
my gender is
overthinking
my labels
dangle like
loose teeth:
Girl
Boy
Nonbinary
Dyke
Lesbian
Bisexual
I wait
for certainty to
crawl out of me
Athena leaping
out of my forehead
instead
my
articulation
grows like
hair
lately
I believe
my gender
is
a fountain of blood
in
the shape of
people
I love
and
people
I will never know
11,294
BAK
BAKKER, ELNA
The great Sc
gender
fountains all over
myself
XVIII
I find
stains
in the sheets
I scrub them out
with a toothbrush
their scraggly
outlines remain
sun
-shaped
pennies
lately
my gender is
fear -
what happens
if I relinquish
the power that I find in your eyes? outside
white bears asphyxiate
in plastic boxes
across San Fernando
Cemetery
while pickup trucks
drive by tattooed
with names
of
dead cousins, car clubs
and some
that say
tengo novia toxica
I cut paper to create
new
shapes
at night
fragments
of flora
and faces
are scattered
against
the dining room table
I am trying
to invent
a new context
I am trying
to create
a gender with
what is given to me:
the dyke couple by
the oranges
the sage bush
blooming purple
after the storm
the Little Flower basilica steeple
that slits
the sky open
Yes, it's
the steeple
O
God,
I want to be the steeple.

gender-shape #2

i throw myself at the internet
like a performance piece about

a girl inventing a new way
to be remembered.

i wake up with a blue light hangover.
my Tumblr inbox crowded with ribbons

of tension tethered to men
i will never meet.

i post a GIF from a Radiohead
music video in hopes that they notice.

we dye each other
with our confessional

desire or suicidal thoughts.
i fall in love with so many

of them so often
i can't keep track

except that's not really true.
what i mean is that

i have been infatuated
with so many men

but all i really wanted was
their stamp of desirability

above my eyebrows.
no, that's not right either.

really, i looked at their pictures
and thought, do i want

to be the one pressed up
against their jeans?

or do i want to
be the one pressed up against?

self portrait as my memory of nana's backyard

my mood: the water hose drooling all over
cracked cement
the watery smell
tinting the dusk
my body: the magenta crepe myrtle
shedding all over itself

my brain: Güero barking
at visitors
he has seen hundreds of times
his paws caked in mud

my ideas: a line of terra cotta pots
overflowing with lantanas
and esperanzas
my soul: a stray piece of cascarone confetti
from last Easter, still buried in Saint
Augustine grass

my memory: the dark garage full of fishing rods
children books with silverfish crushed
between its pages
dried up paint cans
with thick tears of baby blue
frozen in time

my wanting: the dragon-shaped bougainvillea
its arms brush the hoods of parked cars
cuidado my tías told me

my fear: overheard conversation from the kitchen
where women talk about
what other women do with their lives
and how its always wrong

my longing: pecans from the tree in the back
wobbling on the kitchen table,
waiting to turn into
some
thing sweet

sky

it is not until an out-of-state friend says:
the sky is so big here

that i remember how big this sky can be.
i think of the cowboy i met in Terlingua.

when a friend asked why he moved there,
he pointed upwards and said, *this.*

i think of San Marcos sunsets above the H-E-B parking
lot: orange and red spread against blue-gray toast i think

of those spring break afternoons in March's throat,
visiting Sterling in Dallas. the sun's glow on my eyelids

while i laid on my back and i thought of You.
oh, that week in Dallas. i scrambled

eggs in Sterling's apartment while she
was in class, learning about childhood development.

in the evenings Sterling and i watched gay men
pole dance with angel wings on. our mornings spent

in the well-watered campus grass while i read her copy of *A*
Little Life—every moment, every memory was as big

as this state, where hours away You were falling
back in love with Your Ex.

oh, this week in my memory is the smell
of Replica's Jazz Club, red and pink streamers

in the Thai restaurant, my short hair and
red scarf at the lesbian bar, your text,

i love you like milkweed loves Summer.
two Aprils after this one, Your mother

would read Your poem at Your
Zoom memorial. i cannot be mad

at You anymore. when i was a child,
i thought the second coming of Jesus

would include a reel of every second
of my life, projected on the sky for all

my family to see. the thought used to
keep me up. now, i would do anything

to watch these Dallas afternoons
like a movie against a Texas sunset.

i don't care anymore,
show all my footage on a cloud.

there is no more time
for shame.

Having a Lone Star with You

after Frank O'Hara & Liz Plair's "Fuck and Run"

is sexier than sleeping with you.
i lean across the table and steal
your Miller High Life and i hand you
my tall red and white aluminum body.
the doormen shout but right now,
it's only us.

green light halos our buzzing flesh.
your jean jacket, my tight black skirt.
our fingers seared with the smell of tobacco.
buttons of my blouse clamoring
to be undone. the roof drips with desire
and roads are full of stretch marks.

before the lights come on, we kiss to
"Wicked Game" like it's 1989 and i'm glinting like
a blue heart-shaped balloon. in the morning, all i
want is to be back at the bar, itching for salt in the
mouth. i'd rather have you there, bending towards
me, opening your feelings for me

like a gift in front of a crowd.

constellation-shape

the first boy i liked was Alex. i wrote his name all over my bedroom floor in red crayon. i drew a portrait of us in front of our square-shaped house and hid it in the back of my sock drawer.

i bought cherry-flavored beer and listened to R.E.M.'s first album on the day before I met M. we met on the bar patio flushed with red neon. he tells me the people he admires the most are all teachers.

i loved W but he was still in love with his ex. that autumn, i sat by the San Marcos River and lit red candles. I notebook papered a spell with K's name on it. i ask the stars to bind him to me.

M broke up with me over diner pie, weeks after i broke his trust. i threw myself at someone new, in hopes of forgetting my shame—we danced to Willie Hutch until we were in line at Waffle House. all that's left of W is a picture of him from across the table, my grandmother's red scarf tied around his neck while he looks into his water cup.

it has been five Decembers since i poured wax onto K's ribs. we took turns until i could no longer kiss the lighter to the wick. my bedroom was a b movie horror movie set, a broken ruby, a ripped up valentine, a tiger's blood raspa.

i look at the past now—what was once the cigarette's cherry glowing in the dark is now ash in the backyard grass. i grieve the ghosts of men i know i no longer want.

witness

i'm leaning on my balcony railing where there is hardly
any light. i hold a red candle and look at a polaroid of us,

asking the stars to extract my want into the real world.
let me spit it out like a cherry pit.

all i want to listen to is your go to
karaoke song. my memories of you are stubborn.

i always return to that night in November
when my hair was freshly bleached and

we danced to Jonathan Richman.
you threw an empty Lone Star

across the parking lot and it flew like a comet.
our reservations peeled away on the walk to your car.

bodies pressed up against car seat vinyl.
your protruding bones illuminated by

high pressure sodium lamps.
ribs as rigid as saguaro cacti.

the names of couples carved into skinny trees
were like voyeurs and for that i was thankful.

more than i wanted you,
i wanted a witness.

gender-shape #3

i can't stop looking at myself
in every
reflective surface
obsessed with
my shape at every angle
where sex spills out of me
where it is sewn up

i am waiting to feel
innocuous

i fantasize about
dipping myself in
gender, today
i am a long gray sunset
cloud that hovers
above the H-E-B parking lot
tomorrow,
i will be Texas
wild rice in Sewell Park
today, red and white
toothpaste hardens
on the sink's lip reminding me
that cleaning is overdue
nana's earrings sits
on the bathroom counter

their backings like

golden cockroach legs

reflecting on a butch's tattoo in the chinese takeout line

i am jealous of how you love
from wrist to elbow in fat calligraphy:

a tattoo of woman's name
that i can't recall now
it could have been your tía,
your nana, your daughter or a label-less love

you spent hours in the spirals
of someone's name

do you ever raise your arm and spot
the tail of your beloved's last letter

– a gray snake motionless, nearly kissing
the mountain of your elbow

are all your memories
amber-colored too

underneath your Astros hat
your hair — a neat fade like the boys

i used to teach last spring
your t-shirt — as long as my dress

your basketball shorts and silver hoops
not unlike the ones She wore

when i first met her —
we talk race and gender

on weeknights — coffee
and weed in hand, we never said

anything about what we did
in the dark, our attraction was

silent, like your beloved's name
shining in the dull light

of the Chinese take out line
on a Thursday night

outside, wind blows a plastic bag
to somewhere darker

than here

summer on w. summit

while you water our peach tree – you point out how the light turns green leaves neon – while I lasso my house of feeling – I am reminded of the long summer hours when chicharras let me know it was time for dinner – a trail of water swam towards the street – my grandmother's backyard full of plants I wish I remembered – once we found a clear quartz geode – I saw myself in the future – but it was full of clouds – pecans sitting in the burnt autumn blades – we crack them open on the kitchen table – in the late fall – a nearby church festival rises up like a slow sunset – we get our goldfish prizes and go home – sad orange stars swimming in circles – raspas down the block from nana's house – tigers blood with ice cream on top – the AC unit whirring into the night – while the train two houses down rattles the windows—

unbury the light

God's nighttime cigarette
clouds the stars to death.

a trail of red lights blink as
they wait to turn onto Culebra road.

today, i showed students how to identify
theme in a story and reminded them

to write in full sentences
inside, i'm dying because i fail

to see the point. at the long red light,
my mind flips through the rolodex

of my weekend. i think about
my brown friend's research

about lenten salmon patties—
reminding me of the yellow walls

in my nana's kitchen,
her ceramic roosters staring

as she scrapes salmon from the pan.
the peach fuzz of her face glowing

in the April afternoon light.
did she overanalyze her life

while soaking dishes in hot sink water?
was her mind a long distance runner

or did she not find the time to think?
did she ever feel endlessly sad

while selling jewels downtown
or decorating wedding cakes?

did she keep her thoughts to herself
like a quartz glowing beneath the dirt?

or is it just that overthinking
is my luxury to live with?

september 2021

something tightens inside me
like a braid pulled tight at the root.
i start missing all of the times
where i was hedonistic and preoccupied
with maximizing my likability
chicharras sing like elegant car
alarms outside the living room window.
i wish on the late Texas sky—
to be sad again before all
this global sickness.
i don't remember everything
but it's hard to forget how i felt.
i want to wake up and feel
a little less hopeless.
i google questions
with no real answers
while the backyard white sage
grows in silence.
right now, i am grateful
that i can mention the death
of Yolanda Lopez and my friends will
know exactly who i am talking about. i
feel so much pressure to enjoy
every autumn because the next one
will be different.
my braid of memory crushes me
like soft petals of geraniums between
the tissue paper pages of my father's
dictionary, flattened but still full of color.

black stones

i stare at the mug's indentations on my tía's vinyl tablecloth as she tells me about my great great great someone, a general en Piedras Negras, known for giving the gold buttons off his jacket to los pobres en las calles. *he was known as a very giving man* my tía says. / it i's funny how death seals up the throats of the living. we can't stop baptizing the dead into saints. / a pre-colonial mural haunts me at the Tex Mex restaurant—a woman with a white nose and tiny waist carried in the arms of an Aztec warrior. a brown woman wearing bamboo knockers pours coffee in my cup. / tonight, the moon is a black stone. i fail to find stars above the city light. i burn bay leaves with one word affirmations. the sky swallows up my tokens of smoke like dollars to a godly vending machine. if only it was as easy as offering ancient blessings while my spiritual prize clangs around until it is ready for the taking. / where did all the wishes of my ancestors go? / what memory of me will play in someone's head before i die for the final time?

La Lechuza at Woodlawn Lake Park

how can I say it other than this:
I am no worse than you

I do what I need
for survival

I watch families
from tree branches
half as ancient as I am

Bad Bunny's voice swirls
through the air

while an ice cream truck
makes itself known

a child at a picnic table
looks up at me and knows
there are bad things to come

I leave before his tías flock
to wrap their arms around him

the women always know
how to get rid of me

their birthday party
blurs below me

Everyone you love will die.
A storm will destroy your home.
what use are my omens?

my life is wasted on telling
you what you have already imagined.

january 2018

the vultures are always circling high above my body. they
circle me when i listen to Frank Ocean on cold days,

when i grip the ends of my dress and my burgundy beret,
when i sit cross legged and alone, drinking a hot toddy.

they were there when i became more than a somebody to you on
that Friday. i sat on your kitchen counter
and finally you flayed my heart. i want to tattoo

that moment on my thigh: i asked for a Diet Coke and whiskey
while i traced the scars on your back. curtains hiked up, revealing

the wet windy night.
in those early hours, i admired how

your shoulders resembled a wire hanger
bent with the weight of a heavy coat. yes,

the vultures witnessed our bodies enshrined
by green sheets and stars like La Virgen.

they circled above me while i drove in daylight,
back to my love sleeping in my second story apartment.

i felt like a dagger and prayed to the vultures to take me apart
and scatter pieces of myself for you to find.

central texas seance

i have tried to summon
your mania
that used to trickle down your forehead

i try to light a candle
but my lighter doesn't reach
the wick

i read Denise Levertov's "The Prayer"
and think of your scratchy voice reciting,
I drank of the brackish
spring there
while winter hardened
pecan trees outside

i play *Feel Like Making Love* by Marlena Shaw
the song you showed me

while dozens of little lights bent
around familiar corners
on our drive home
air whipped against our faces
i sopped up Marlena's voice
and your lipsync
like a drag queen

i don't think
my prayers reach you

i close my eyes
and watch our last small moment at the Big H-E-B,

pieces missing in my mind except
your brown rectangle glasses
that matched your hair
and the colors
of the Holistic Health aisle
the first time I called your spirit
was in late May:

i sat with Melanie on the Hays Street Bridge
eating sour gummy worms
while the sky blackened

all i got was
a silent hour
you ignore me from
the other side
of the veil

maybe i am naive in trying
to summon you

maybe it is enough
to realize the urgency
of my dreams of you
long before we kissed:

our hands gently touching
in nighttime
parking lot light

do my dreams make sense
to you too?

sometimes i think
it's not you who's listening

but another god
something crueler

friend-shape

for Clint

night ashes itself
                    while we walk around
your father's neighborhood
                    full of silence & white rocks
the land was pregnant with wood, stone, and dirt
          the houses must be alive by now
we crunch grass
          and sip our beers, like quakers
we don't speak unless the lord
                              of language moves us
discomfort does not live here
          we walk by the community college
lamps brighten the sidewalk's lines
          i want to hold on to what has left
that this poem is a spell to bring it all
                      back to me

i've been meaning to

conduct some plant magic, like my astrologer suggested
my chart says i have a knack for necromancy too,

maybe that's true through language – i don't know
how to not talk about dead things – my grandmother –

barbie computer games – cliff bars i bought at the corner
store on my way to work at the university – the hole

in ceiling of my childhood bedroom – i excel at forgetting
about the plants i own – my good habits last a week

before sadness seeps into my pores when i'm sleeping

flower talk

we talk about flower sex
look at illustrations on science sites and
learn about outcrossers – flowers that
have both reproductive systems but still
can be incompatible with oneself

i have only understood myself
through incompatibility
with myself

the moments i feel best
about myself are the times
when i forget i have a body

like yesterday, we discreetly
pee in the river while a couple
gets married on the hill nearby

and everybody cheers

picking up margarita mix on new year's eve

feeling innocuous
i watch a man walk out
of the liquor store
a palm-sized bottle

i project my misery
onto him
and drive home

this day feels no different
from the rest – i am always
thinking about my past

and when i see it
it is quiet sunlight
on the sidewalk
puddles outside
the dive bar

longing was
my first language

how can i get back
to standing under
the pecan trees
of my childhood

re-converse
on a crosswalk
with people
i hardly know

those fridays in high school
i spent with my father
who took me to half price books
where i inhaled dust
and found *Let It Bleed* on vinyl

janus, can you teach me
how to hold onto comfort?

like a hot tortilla on the comal, my brain bloats with longing

how else can i say that i want to be everything?
fuzzy spanish dialogue from the tiny tv
on the kitchen counter while papas sizzled
on nana's stove

Juania's dreams described scene by scene
after we decide to spend the day indoors

my first girlfriend's bedroom skylight
leaking early blue light on us in
the midst of figuring out our feelings

hours after a lover's betrayal, the bar
with friends and the walk home to a friend's
apartment where she showed me her nighttime
skincare ritual

looking at seagulls with my beloved
in Corpus Christi, high & eating sandwiches,
the sun bleaching our brains clean of any thoughts

Sterling and i reading Leslie Jamison's memoir
to each other at the park and then at the diner

singing "Doll Parts" with Amber on a Monday night
at the now closed down gay bar

watching *Mysterious Skin* on my laptop, Clint walking in
with a tray of bagel bites and blue powerade

the pool tables and jukebox at Cat's,
haven't i said this before?
that color of Spanish rice on the stove. my mother's
Sade CD on heavy rotation.

can't you see the color of my soul?

love poem

riding in my mother's car, stuck in traffic
she dropped me off so i wouldn't have to park,

showing her love for me after her birthday dinner
i missed your set by minutes

and waited for you to come back from your car
putting away your guitar,

i was sad in my trench coat
i fell in love with your long hair,

brown leather jacket, we kissed in cold air
like we did weeks ago on our first date by the river

the river we've walked by a handful of times
sometimes in silence, punctuated by *oh babys*

just yesterday we sat under a bridge by Confluence Park and
watched two teenage boxers across the water

filmed by their friends on the sidelines
we sipped our watermelon and pineapple aguas frescas

we go home and watch drag queens on TV
with you it is easy to forget the complications

like how empire can run our blood cold—

apology to my past selves

the time i sat in my parents' backyard
two weeks after i came back from Spain

i thought i had reached the end of joy
my brain sucked the root juice of memory

that one night in Alcala de Henares
arm in arm with Sofia walking home

from the Mexican-themed bar
we stopped at a playground behind the mall

Sofia played Lua from her phone speakers
we were eager to be sad

about anything
commiseration as prayer

we hardly knew each other then
but we tried our best to learn

about each other and our thoughts
on Picasso's *Guernica*

to be honest, i don't know
if that all happened

in the same night but
i wanted to tell you

something linear – i want to trace
a constellation from beginning to end

and what i really want to say is
i still make the same mistake of thinking

i have reached the end of it all
it has always been hard for me

to see the future as anything other
than darkness

after that night in the backyard,
i have had my ecstatic days

and my losses too
yesterday i went to get coffee with a friend

white capitalized letters
spelled out words like LONDON

FOG and FRENCH PRESS on the menu
a bird almost pooped on my shoe

while light turned leaves chartreuse
and that night, i watched shadow

fill up my beloved's pores
i put my past selves to sleep,

telling them: *i am sorry, i am sorry*
there was no way i could have known

it could get better

Notes

Thank you to the following literary journals that published many of the poems in this book:

1. "Self Portrait as an Anna Karina GIF at 17" – *The Los Angeles Review*, 2023
2. "I Feel like an Antonioni Movie" – *Prairie Schooner*, 2023
3. "Eternal Life," "What I Know" – *Latino Horror Stories*, Arte Publico Press, 2023
4. "Filth-Shaped" – *Sybil Journal*, 2024
5. "I am always wanting other lives" – *wildness*, 2021
6. "Gender-Shape" – *The Boiler*, 2024
7. "Unburying the Light" – *Voices de la Luna*, 2022
8. "Central Texas Seance" – *Occulum*, 2023
9. "September" – *Voices de la Luna*, 2022
10. "Sky" – *Escritorio Purgatorio*, Plancha Press, 2023
11. "the past is a jean jacket" – *the winnow*, 2022

Acknowledgments

This book would not be possible without the emotional support from the Infrarrealistas: Juania Sueños, Amber Isaac, Dee Lalo Garcia, and SG Huerta. Y'all mean everything to me.

Thank you to my family, Jacinto Jesús Cardona, Olga Garza Cardona, and Andres Cardona for their love and support. I wouldn't be a poet without y'all!

Thank you to my tías, Norma Garza, and Maria Smalling aka Loops. I would also like to thank the Garza family. I am grateful for all of your love and support.

Thank you to all of my friends across Texas and beyond: Aaron Arguello, Claire Bowman, Diamond Braxton, KB Brookins, Carmen Calatayud, Bonnie Cisneros, Abby Cothran, Clint Dierker, Violeta Garza, Tammy Gonzales, Saúl Hernández, Chan Krishna, Maria Maloney, Molly Moltzen, Jacob Moore, Natalia Mujadzic, Ariana Ortiz, mónica teresa ortiz, Sebastian H. Páramo, Dr. Sara A. Ramirez, Reyes Ramirez, Sofia Ramos, Jorge Antonio Renaud, jo reyes-boitel, Sterling Richards, Kristine Robb, Melanie Robinson, Pamela Santiago, Camille Sauers, James Soto, Natalia Treviño, Leticia Urieta, Annar Veröld, Gazzmine Wilkins, and Sofía Zanetta. My art wouldn't be possible without you. I also want to shout out all the friends I've met on Tumblr throughout the years. This book wouldn't exist without y'all.

Thank you to all my teachers: Gabrielle Bates, Cyrus Cassells, Cyra Dumitru, Geneva Gano, Naomi Shihab Nye, Cecily Parks, Kathleen Peirce, and Ito Romo.

Thank you to all the lovely folks at Gemini Ink: Joshua Cantú, Florinda Flores-Brown, Alexandra van de Kamp, Anisa Onofre, Catherine Burianek, and Mandy Lynn.

Thank you to the organizations that have empowered me to write: Letras Latinas, Macondo Writing Workshop, and Tin House Writers Workshop. I especially want to shout out Francisco Aragón, Laura Villarreal, and Brent Ameneyro.

Many thanks to the wonderful team at Hub City Press. I especially want to thank Kate McMullen, Julie Jarema, and Jae Nichelle. Thank you all for believing in my work!

Thank you to Embroidery by Claudia, who made the jacket I'm wearing on the cover.

Finally, I would like to thank Sadie. Thank you for all of your love.

PUBLISHING
New & Extraordinary
VOICES FROM THE
AMERICAN SOUTH

HUB CITY PRESS is a non-profit independent press in Spartanburg, SC that publishes well-crafted, high-quality works by new and established authors, with an emphasis on the Southern experience. We are committed to high-caliber novels, short stories, poetry, plays, memoir, and works emphasizing regional culture and history. We are particularly interested in books with a strong sense of place.

Hub City Press is an imprint of the non-profit Hub City Writers Project, founded in 1995 to foster a sense of community through the literary arts. Our metaphor of organization purposely looks backward to the nineteenth century when Spartanburg was known as the "hub city," a place where railroads converged and departed.

The Hub City Press BIPOC Poetry Series was created to spotlight poetry by writers working in the American South, writing about BIPOC communities. Two finalists were selected by Editor-at-Large Ashley M. Jones.The Hub City Press BIPOC Poetry Series is open to poets of all stages of their careers who reside in or are from the South and self-identify as a member of a Southern BIPOC community. This series is made possible with funding from the Poetry Foundation.

BIPOC PRIZE HONOREES

2025: *the past is a jean jacket* Cloud Delfina Cardona

2026: *black frag/ments* Lolita Stewart-White